SING FREEDOM!

SONGS OF SOUTH AFRICAN LIFE

Collected, transcribed and edited by Margaret Hamilton

In memory of James Madhlope Phillips who devoted his life in exile to sharing the soul of South Africa through the songs of the people

and

Dedicated to courageous friends in South Africa committed to liberation and peace

Foreword by
Archbishop Desmond Tutu

GW00646809

NOVELLO PUBLISHING LIMITED
8/9 Frith Street, London W1V 5TZ

Christian Aid
P.O. Box 100, London, SE1 7RT

Order No: NOV 070528

Cover picture by

Martin Stevens

of the Community Arts Project, Cape Town

A cassette of 21 songs from **Sing Freedom!**, sung by Kopanang, is available from
Counterpoint, One World Desk, Christain Aid Office, Carrs Lane, Church Centre,
Birmingham, B4 7SX, UK (tel: 021 643 2249).

ISBN 0-85360-158-5

Foreword

What a gift God has given us in music! Particularly in making our own music; in singing everyone can participate. Music has the power to touch people in a way that words never can. Whether it is by listening to those who sing, or by joining in song together.

It has the power to stir the emotions, to speak to a lover, to praise God, to raise courage, to inspire hope, to console. In South Africa we have been singing songs of hope. Those of our mother tongue and those that we have borrowed and made our own from other liberation movements. 'We Shall Overcome' stirs us as it has stirred our sisters and brothers in the United States. We welcome the opportunity through this book of being able to share some of these songs and stories with a wider number of people around the world.

Too often now we are singing with tears in our eyes as we mourn the death of yet more innocent victims of the violence that has become endemic in our beautiful, but sad and bleeding land. When is it all going to stop? We keep having to be wiping tears from people's eyes.

Through music may we keep hope alive. May it help us hold on to our faith that whatever the appearance to the contrary, God really is in charge, it is His world. Righteousness and goodness will overcome evil and oppression, and we shall all be free, black and white together.

God Bless you

✠ Desmond Cape Town

25 September 1992

CONTENTS

INTRODUCTION

'Your God will conquer for you'

Where there is oppression there are songs of liberation. This has been the case from as far back at least as the days of the Israelites in Egypt, and in the last 100 years resistance songs have been sung by Afrikaners suffering repression by the British, by Indians under the Raj, by African-Americans and by those who struggle for justice and peace in Latin America, the Philippines, Southern Africa and many other countries too. With the intensification of repression in South Africa these songs became particular signs of the times and never more so than after the effective banning in February 1988 of the 17 organisations which were the main mouthpieces of the people, resulting in a mushrooming of People's Culture as groups expressed their anger, fears and hopes in drama, art and music.

But the struggle is not only a political one in the narrow sense; it is on all levels of life. It is struggle for existence in a shack in Mshenguville, Soweto; in a corrugated iron hut in Rooigrond in the homeland of Bophuthatswana; under canvas as an evicted farm-worker in Weenen, Natal. It is struggle against poor sanitation and impure water and the resulting sickness that claims unnecessarily high numbers of black lives each year. It is struggle for education when black schools are ill-equipped and when homework has to be done by candle-light in a crowded 4-room matchbox house. It is struggle to find money for food when there is no work in a system which protects jobs for whites and gives no State benefits to the unemployed; to keep a family together or to raise children as a single parent because the father is forced to work thousands of miles away as a migrant labourer. It is struggle to preserve a sense of dignity and worth as a human being, to resist internalizing the propaganda that to be black is to be inferior; to retain the qualities of humanity, to refuse to hate, to shun despair, to laugh, to be loving and especially forgiving, to be prepared to be vulnerable. It is struggle to maintain faith in God and to understand the ways in which God is working in South Africa today. Small wonder then that when I explained I was collecting songs that reflected people's lives and experiences I was then introduced to the next person with the words: 'This is Maggie. She's collecting songs of the struggle'.

South Africa is a country that groans and travails in its yearning for liberation, for salvation. How can human beings combat evil and remain true to their faith in God and Jesus Christ as the Prince of Peace? The Christian Church in South Africa consistently advocates active resistance through non-violent means and promotes the gospel of love and peace with justice. However, just as many Christians in Europe felt not only morally justified but also compelled to take up arms to stop the evil of Hitler's regime, either within State structures of the armed forces or less formally as in the French Resistance, so there have been those in South Africa who, recognizing the magnitude of the evil confronting them, have felt the only effective means of eliminating it and gaining freedom to be recourse to armed struggle. Such decisions, never made easily, were only made at all because of earlier intransigence on the part of the South African government and the international community alike to take major effective measures to bring about the end of apartheid. So in South Africa there has been no paradox in committed Christians singing liberation songs supporting the armed struggle and also songs which bear testimony to their steadfast faith in God.

On arrival in South Africa in July 1989 the stringent Emergency regulations imposed in June 1986 were still in force. But countering these was the growth of resistance in the Defiance Campaign surrounding the September General Election (in which only 2% of the population voted). By the time I left in late October the pressure on De Klerk to achieve a rescheduling of foreign debt repayments and to deflect pressure for sanctions at the Commonwealth Summit in Kuala Lumpur had resulted in a new semblance of tolerance; eight political

2 prisoners had been released and several marches and protests had been allowed to take place, albeit after earlier protests had been brutally broken up. Since then, the African National Congress (ANC) and other restricted and banned organizations have been unbanned and Nelson Mandela has been released. Although there have been welcome alterations in some structures of apartheid over the last year, life at grassroots continues much as before. Recent discussions have given hope for a negotiated change, but it is clear that the wall of apartheid and its legacy will take much longer to dismantle than that which for 30 years marred the view through the Brandenburg Gate.

NOTE

Most of the songs in this collection are generally regarded as songs of the people and as such are unpretentious, with no particular claim to 'musical greatness' as it is interpreted in the West, although much beauty and life lies in them. The purpose of their inclusion in this book is to present some aspects of South African life as it is experienced in the raw, allowing the voices of people rarely heard to speak, or rather sing, for themselves. Considerable effort has been made to ensure the accuracy of texts and translations, whilst recognizing regional variations that occur. Thanks are offered to Jean Benjamin for permission to reproduce her songs. Every attempt has been made to ascertain copyright owners and the compiler apologizes to any whose rights have inadvertently not been acknowledged.

ACKNOWLEDGEMENTS

Many people have contributed towards making this book possible. Special thanks are due to the Joseph Rowntree Charitable Trust for funding the visit to South Africa through the Community for Reconciliation; to Jane Alderson and Anne Hughes at Christian Aid; Leslie East at Novello; the Christian Fellowship Trust; Joan and John Johansen-Berg; Marguerite Mae CSC; James Madhlope Phillips and Donald Swann.

Above all, deep thanks are due to the many people in South Africa, from all different backgrounds, cultures and faiths, who gave so much of themselves, their stories and songs, sometimes at personal risk to themselves. Their courage, integrity, love and faith remain a constant inspiration. I thank especially the office- and field-workers of the South African Council of Churches and the Wits, West Rand and Western Province Councils of Churches; the Congress of South African Trade Unions and affiliated unions, particularly SACTWU and SADWU; the Institute of Contextual Theology; all the churches I visited, in particular St Paul's Jabavu, Youth Alive and the Methodist Church in Soweto, and Ebenezer Evangelical Church in Mohlakeng; PACSA; Diakonia; Mandla at AFRA; Sizanani; the Natal Organization of Women; the Culture and Working Life Project in Durban, especially Nise Malange and Cleo Ehlers; students at the University of Western Cape and Stellenbosch; MAPP; and many individuals including Lawrencia Askham, Jean Benjamin, Sue Brittion, Revd Harold Brookes, Mr A. S. and Mrs Saras Chetty, Peter and Joan Kerchoff, Revd Tom Mbabane, Dudu Modise, Dorothy Motubatse, Ilse and Beyers Naude, Esther Rejoice Ndaba, Revd David Newby, Khumo and Moss Ntla, all who provided words and translations for the songs I recorded and those who generously offered me hospitality.

Maggie Hamilton, December 1991

PERFORMANCE NOTES

1. These transcriptions are skeletal, for every verse of every song is different with free solo embellishments and often altered harmonies. In addition, there are regional differences in the performance of a song.
2. Performance practice should be uninhibited, with body movements, hand-clapping and vocal extemporization.
3. A good sense of rhythm is essential and much of what appears to be on the beat in fact anticipates it slightly.
4. Musicians beware! You will be sorely tempted to 'correct' discrepancies in the harmonies in accordance with the rules of Western European music theory, to change a note here and there to make it 'fit' in with the chord, to eliminate consecutive fifths and octaves, to fill in the absent third of a chord. Although the transcriptions are frameworks on which to build, the alterations mentioned above will erode the true sound and spirit of the songs; each change will be a move towards a reproduction of *Hymns Ancient and Modern*.

PRONUNCIATION

In the African languages this is easier than might be imagined, being in the main literal vocalizing of the letters without the subtleties of eliding two letters like *t* and *h* (*th* would be pronounced as though separate, i.e. *t* followed by an aspiration, not as in the English *th*). Similarly *ph* is not like an *f* but rather a *p h*. However, *sh* remains as in English. Exceptions are:

hl is pronounced as in the Welsh *ll* (e.g. *Llanberis*).

x is pronounced as a clicking sound, as in geeing up a horse.

q is pronounced as a hard clucking sound (the tongue far back on the roof of the mouth).

c is pronounced as in a 'tut' sound.

s in Sotho songs is pronounced as a very light *sh*, like a kettle on the gas.

g is sometimes pronounced with a slight guttural sound (like *ch* in *loch*).

Often the final syllable is lost in the singing, and earlier syllables are run together. Where this occurs, a note is appended to the song.

Pronunciation notes for the Afrikaans and Hindi songs appear in the text.

TEACHERS' NOTES

1. Although these songs are normally sung unaccompanied, guitar symbols have been added to allow for a harmonic and rhythmic accompaniment when the songs are to be sung in unison or two parts only.
2. The simplicity of many of the tunes makes them suitable to be played on glockenspiels, recorders or other melodic instruments with optional guitar and additional percussion.
3. Some of the melodies are memorable enough to be taught by rote. The remaining parts can be added on other pitched instruments.
4. The teacher or an individual pupil can play the leader line. These especially give scope for extemporization within the harmonic framework.

CHURCH SONGS

In the past the Church played an ambivalent role in the politics of South Africa. The Dutch Reformed Church (DRC) was instrumental in setting up separate churches for congregations of different colour groups in response to white members refusing to share the communion cup with non-whites. It tried to support theologically the State's policy of apartheid and denounced resistance to this as being against the will of God. (This view was reversed officially by the DRC at the Rustenburg Conference in November 1990, although some churches privately refuse to accept this change in attitude.) Other mainstream denominations were less openly active in supporting apartheid but nonetheless endorsed it tacitly by their reluctance to speak out against it.

Notable individual exceptions include Fr Trevor Huddleston, who exercised a legendary ministry in Sophiatown before the forced removals; Beyers Naudé and the Christian Institute; and certain other ministers who spoke out and acted prophetically. After the banning of the Institute the new South African Council of Churches and their regional Councils took on much work in trouble-shooting for the oppressed, protecting their rights, caring for families of detainees and working for justice and reconciliation on both the political and grassroots levels in the townships. But only in the 1980s has a more concerted body of South African churches taken the side of the poor.

Church leaders such as Archbishop Desmond Tutu, Revd Dr Allan Boesak, Revd Frank Chikane, Fr Smangaliso Mkatshwa and others have spoken openly and fearlessly not only to denounce apartheid as a heresy and to call for justice but also to sow the seeds for a genuine and lasting peace within the country. Liberation theologians have encouraged the oppressed to read the Bible with fresh understanding and some churches express this in their worship and liturgy.

In 1985 the Kairos Document, a critique of the theologies of State and Church, called for a prophetic theology relevant to the South African situation. After the State of Emergency was declared in 1986 church services became the only legal meeting points for large numbers of people, drawing some churches into a deeper involvement in the struggle. Since then there has been growing prophetic witness in delegations, marches, public protests, congregational links and the Standing for the Truth campaign in 1989 in which Christians participated in large numbers in the Mass Democratic Movement protest actions. The church has consequently regained some of its credibility among young people, many of whom had regarded it as at best ineffectual and at worst a pillar of the system. A student said: 'We are grateful for the role that has been played and continues to be played by the Church in the struggle itself. The Church has fully identified with the aspirations of our people - the Church has been there sharing our suffering.... It has been a beacon of hope and a great source of strength for our people.'

Although the Church is now united in declaring its opposition to apartheid, there are still differences of understanding about legitimate ways of opposing it. The majority would support all non-violent strategies internally and externally in the form of sanctions, boycotts and other economic pressures. Most would not support the armed struggle or other uses of violent force regardless of the justice of the cause, understanding the way of Christ to be that of non-violent resistance, overcoming evil with love. Some however understand the armed struggle as entirely biblical; a Roman Catholic nun saw it as God's way of establishing His Kingdom on earth, of bringing in His peace and justice, drawing parallels with the Bible: 'A person must resist evil. In the book of Judges the restoration of the land was not so peaceful. The Bible is a book of resistance.... The resistance is the process of reconciliation.... If I love you I confront you and call you to be above what you are.'

Certainly if one ever accepts the 'just war' theory and the use of violence in the sustaining of a nation's armed forces, then the use of arms cannot be denounced out of hand in the context of the liberation struggle in South Africa. Some have found that oppression has brought them to a deeper, stronger faith as they have stepped out with courage in hope and experienced God present with them in a powerful way. Others have been left struggling with their faith and the effects of detention have left some broken. No-one's faith is able to stand still.

On the whole the songs sung in the mainstream denominations are a mixture of indigenous songs and European hymns translated into the appropriate African language. Old missionary hymnbooks are common, such as *Songs from Zion,* used at a memorial service in Zeerust for people killed following the incorporation of two villages into Bophuthatswana. *Monateng Kapele* is a univerally known church song full of assurance about meeting in heaven, and the spontaneous singing of it reflected the courage and indomitable spirit rising again after months of trauma and a day in which the original service in Braklaagte had been banned and we had been turned out of Bophuthatswana by extremely angry soldiers rattling their rifle triggers.

Although well-meaning, some direct translations retaining the European tune have changed the intonation of the African language and resulted in nonsensical alterations in the meaning of the original text. An attempt to overcome this difficulty was made committedly by Fr Dave Dargie, a white Roman Catholic priest working for the Lumko Missiological Institute. Xhosa composition workshops for African church musicians have already produced several books containing over 600 new church songs, some accompanied by traditional instruments such as the uhadi (musical bow), and others by the vibrant tones of marimbas.

Church songs in the townships are usually sung unaccompanied, regardless of their origin, due to the scarcity of organs in African churches. However, the congregation sing harmonies to the European hymns from tonic sol-fa or improvise harmonies for the African songs, so there is a fullness of sound including variations and extemporisations in each verse. The only accompaniment is likely to be someone beating time on a plastic-covered kneeler.

The independent churches are divided between those strongly influenced by American Evangelical styles, using imported Charismatic choruses, and those which over the years have developed a predominantly African style of worship including indigenous music. This music itself varies stylistically, some of it referring to the subtler rhythms and harmonies of rural music whilst the majority of songs bear more relation to the tonal and rhythmic qualities of urban music.

The inextricable binding together of faith and life in South Africa is reflected in many church songs which could best be described as 'liberation theology songs' such as *Inzima lendlela* (This road is heavy) and *Thula sizwe* (Be silent, nation), both of which are sung all over South Africa. Others may be a bold affirmation of faith despite the hardships of life, such as *Tumelo yaka* (I will never give up my faith) and *Uthando lwakhe* (God's love is a fascinating mystery). The cutting edge of the gospel is reflected in *Hamba vangeli* (Go, spread the word) and a prayer for the power of the Holy Spirit is seen in the invocation *Tshollela moya wa hao* (Pour down your Spirit). Esther Rejoice Ndaba, at St Paul's Anglican Church, Jabavu (in Soweto), shared with me her favourite song, *Abasundu nabamhlope,* which reflects the universality of Christ and the attitude most commonly found in South Africa, namely a desire that all people can live together in harmony, whatever their colour. The song *Thuma mina* (Send me, Lord) is one of the most popular church songs and the mixture of languages found in it is not uncommon in a country where church services are often held in more than one language, reflecting the integration of black society in a way that has been belied by the

State when they have insisted that tribal differences preclude integration. Finally, the song *Nkosi sikelel' iAfrika* (God bless Africa), composed in 1897 by Enoch Sontonga, is both a hymn and the true national anthem of South Africa, where to sing it has been regarded as an act of defiance. It is sung in other Southern African countries as a token of solidarity.

CHILDREN'S AND YOUTH SONGS

The chasm between the lives of white and black children in South Africa has been well documented over the years. Statistics of infant mortality, disease, malnutrition and poverty cry out in accusation against the government, as do records of inadequate educational facilities and unjust regulations, eventually leading to Sowetan student resistance in 1976, mass school boycotts and even the burning down of some schools. The crisis came to a head after the State of Emergency was announced in 1986 and over the following twelve months or so many children were arrested and detained without charge. Altogether during the period 1984-86 an estimated 11,000 children were detained without trial. Such action provoked international condemnation and pressure for their release. It was also the catalyst for the 1987 Harare Conference 'Children, Repression and the Law in Apartheid South Africa'. Jean Benjamin, who attended, told me: 'The conference found that children in South Africa were not getting the chance to be children; that they were taking on the tasks of adults of transforming the society and in the process they were missing out on a very important phase, which is childhood; and the concern was what kind of adults they were going to be.' Jean captured that dilemma in her song *Stop Killing Our Children*.

The experience of detention, torture and unprovoked violence was evocatively expressed in a children's presentation at a rally in Johannesburg. A choir sang 'Amalungelo ethu sizo walwela - We shall fight for our rights. Even if they detain us, we are prepared to die for our rights.' Later, a dramatic lament depicted police teargassing township children, culminating in the death of one child whose body was carried high by the others to the strain of a solemn song and a drum beat. The transition from childhood to premature adulthood is reflected in the contrast between the simple children's song *Say'ilim'ingqolowa* recorded in a crèche in Meadowlands, Soweto, and the song *Ehlatin'eLusaka* sung by a youth group at a rally in Durban. In a home started by Revd Harold Brookes, the sweet innocence with which farmworkers' children sang *Lerato laJesu* disguised the trauma of their broken homes and lives. This home is now run by a group of dedicated Christians committed to helping to rebuild their lives by expressing the gospel of love.

Within the student bodies there has been growing awareness and organized resistance to the State leading to many students being detained. Some were refused re-entry into State schools under the pretext that they posed a security threat. Such students found themselves unable to complete their education and also to find work for the same reason. Means of alternative education were sought by bodies such as the South African Committee for Higher Education and also by some Councils of Churches.

The Sizanani project was started during the late 1980s by the West Rand Council of Churches to provide final schooling for young people who had been detained. Their quiet application to schoolwork disguised the anger they felt about their experiences in detention; this only emerged in the intensity of the liberation songs they sang in the mid-morning break - *Senzenina* sung with clenched, raised fists; popular songs about the armed struggle, complete with militaristic actions. Once some of them shared their experiences with me, it was easy to understand their aggressive outburst.

Shadrack (16 years old) told of his experiences in detention without charge during which he spent three weeks in solitary confinement and was tortured: 'Some comrades stoned the police and because they know me they came to my place, although I was not there [i.e. when the police were stoned], they bound my hands in the van. When they put me in the room, one was standing behind the door. He tripped me up. My hands were still bound. They put a black sack on my head. Then I felt electric shocks. They were kicking me and trampling on me. When they stopped they turned me over to face the ceiling and one of them walked over me with his boots. He was drunk. They turned me over again and electrocuted me again. When they stopped they hid their instruments so I couldn't see what they were using. They made me stand up but I was so dizzy I fell over and they kicked me again. When I regained consciousness they made me run on the spot. Whilst I was doing this someone hit me again and my head hit a cupboard and started bleeding. Then they made me wash my face and finished interrogating me. The following Monday I was taken to another police station near Johannesburg and they tortured me again'.

These mass detentions effected a brutal politicization of young people which has been expressed in a tough impatience with the slow pace of change in South Africa. One can detect that under the hardness lie many bleeding hearts. Attendance at church involves a search for a God who cares and acts meaningfully in South Africa and the Church has a responsibility to express that in its life and witness. Some churches had organized youth groups which encouraged 'doing theology'; situations common in the townships were reflected on in the light of biblical readings. Two groups I visited had been set up by branches of the independent evangelical churches and I was impressed by the commitment of the young people as we sat in a dark room in Soweto on a cold winter's evening and discussed the Kairos Document by candlelight (due to the constant power failures). The song *Siku rin gwana* was sung by a similar youth group in Ebenezer Evangelical Church in Mohlakeng which had broken away from the mother church who refused to examine the social implications of the gospel. The words could be regarded as pietistic and not addressing the context in which they were sung. However, in seeing that the second coming of Jesus will be cause for celebration because Jesus is on the side of the oppressed, this song takes on an immanent significance in recognizing the God of the poor.

At the higher education level there is even more organized resistance by students in their different unions, resulting in police intervention on campus. The University of the Western Cape has probably been the worst affected by police, who in 1988 and 1989 broke up meetings on campus with tear-gas and live ammunition. The children of a pastor on campus showed me their collection of bullet shells. It was felt that a new form of tear-gas was being used; previously students had protected themselves against its effects by putting wet clothing around their mouths and noses but with the new gas this resulted in burns instead. Students showed great courage in revealing their thoughts considering the constant threat from the security forces.

Resistance understandably did not normally extend itself to Afrikaner universities. One notable exception however was Stellenbosch, where by 1986 there was a branch of the End Conscription Campaign. By the time I visited in September 1989 the police had been on campus three times that year to break up protests about separate accommodation for whites and non-whites, for which the song *Studente sal nooit verloor* was written. Some students were coming to terms with their white background in the overall context of South Africa and had written a number of songs which they had sung on the protests. Some were re-writings of Voortrekker songs, taking cognizance of the fact that the Afrikaners had also had to struggle for their freedom against the British. It is particularly interesting how few words they had to change to make them applicable to South Africa today.

WORK SONGS

Non-whites have historically been regarded as sources of cheap labour throughout our world and although the days of legalized slavery are over there is still a pattern of exploitation today. The bitter pill in South Africa has been that the education system has been specifically designed to keep non-whites in that position and very few have managed to overcome the disadvantages of not being white and enter positions of responsibility and management. The job reservation practice ensured that white people could always find work and the unemployment lists would be almost exclusively of non-whites. After the Land Act of 1913 those who had been used to working their own land before they were dispossessed of it by the State were forced to the towns and cities in search of work and thus became the cheap workforce now operating in most areas of the labour market. The growth of unions was essential to organize workers into taking action to procure just wages and working conditions of which they were deprived by the system of apartheid.

The Group Areas Act and the policy of forced removals in the 1950s prohibited the majority of non-whites from living near their place of work and this was further exacerbated by the creation of 'homelands' into which thousands of blacks were forcibly removed. The homelands provide little employment and so many blacks are compelled to travel for hours each day to get to places of work, such as the night-travellers of Kwa Ndebele who have to leave their homeland towns at 4 or 5 each morning to travel by bus to Pretoria, many of them standing all the way, and who often do not arrive home until 10pm.

For other workers there is not even this option and many are forced to find work hundreds of miles away in 'white' South Africa, in the mines or other national or multi-national concerns. These migrant labourers are away from home for months at a time and live in hostels attached to the mines or situated in the nearest black township to the city where they work. An inevitable result of these policies has been the fragmentation of family life.

Most hostels are bleak and often patrolled by armed guards. The atmosphere was freer in a hostel I visited in the black township of Langa, Cape Town, where women were now allowed to live with their menfolk. There had not been any extension of the premises however; about 500 men lived there, some with their families, and they shared two families to one room. The more open attitude was reflected in the fact that the choirs were mixed as opposed to the male-voice choirs which created the tradition of *iscathamiya* (unaccompanied close-harmony songs) in the mining hostels. A tall Xhosa-speaking bass named Jaca told me that the choirs met three times a week to rehearse diligently for pending competitions and despite the dinginess of their surroundings, with dull brickwork and a solitary bulb lighting the cramped quarters, the singing produced a vibrancy of tone and spirit seldom heard in the West. The choirs sing in English and Xhosa, mainly concentrating on traditional Xhosa rhythms. The song *A ndi bonanga umfana* reflects the rural influence on township culture due to the migrant labour system.

After the formation of the *Congress of South African Trade Unions* (COSATU) late in 1985 the unions became the largest and most powerful voice of resistance to apartheid, especially after the widescale bannings of February 1988. Under circumstances of considerable difficulty, with frequent raids on their offices and harassment of their leaders, the unions have nevertheless succeeded in promoting united organized opposition to injustice within the work structures as well as addressing the wider issues of oppression. Unions that I visited sang two types of song: firstly, workers' songs specifically relating to the trade union movement, when the name of the union would be inserted at the appropriate place (such as *Manyanani basebenzi* and *Klim op die wa*); and secondly, more general songs of protest and liberation which were to be heard all around South Africa.

One of the most difficult unions to set up was that for Domestic Workers. Women employed as full-time domestic workers usually live in a room at the back of the home in a white suburb in order to be on hand for whatever duties are required of them, particularly if they start the day early and/or finish late, because their own homes are miles away in the black townships. This has usually meant that they have not been able to live with their own family, as no spouse or children are allowed to live with them. A hard-hitting line from the play *Inyanga* made this point as the performer, drawing on her own earlier experiences as a domestic worker, started her song, addressed to her employer's son, with the words 'My sister breast-fed my baby while I looked after you'. White employers have often been suspicious of anyone connected with the union so those trying to co-ordinate have sometimes had to overcome abuse, hostility and even dogs being set on them. Despite this, I encountered a strong spirit of determination among domestic workers I met around the country, who shared their joys and sorrows, their love and grief, with a moving openness and vulnerability.

The difficulties of their living conditions were only exceeded by those of farm labourers. The inhuman conditions of life and work of South African farm labourers combined with a growing awareness of the brutality and torture inflicted on them by white farmers prompted the Council of Churches to produce a sticker in 1989 saying 'Farmworkers are God's people too'. Any attempt by the farmworker to question his situation with his employer led to dismissal and consequent eviction, usually reducing the worker and his family to squatting. In addition, farm owners were usually defensive about other people coming onto their farms and had the right to shoot anyone they regard as a trespasser. Even ministers experienced difficulties making pastoral calls. These continuing conditions make it extremely difficult to organize any sort of union or united action by farmworkers, increasing their sense of isolation.

I share now the plight of one such group I visited at Weenen, Natal, who had been evicted from Zypherfontein farm. Mr Zungu's great-grandfather had owned the land and farmed it from 1860, and the family had continued to farm it after it had been taken over by white farmers. Over a period of 3 years all the farmworkers had been evicted and a large number of them were still unhoused and therefore living in tents where they struggled for survival and from which they saw little hope of moving in the near future; runny-nosed children in tatters followed us around with a mixture of awe, excitement and suspicion as we viewed the scene of desolation; overcrowded quarters begged no space for the furniture which had also been moved out and which now stood forlornly by the entrances to the tents, vulnerable to the wind, rain and parching effects of the sun; a couple of women proudly bore a tub of water and a bundle of sticks on their heads; a lame dog chased ankles and some scrawny fowl pecked with undying optimism at the hard ground; and the local council official followed us around, constantly watching, never approaching us, but then questioning the people as soon as we got into the Land Rover to drive away.

Another group had only been moved out the previous month, in July. They sat on the ground outside their tents, shoulders slumped and heads sagging. But nothing more expressed their depression than the fact that they remained seated whilst they sang a song which had arisen from their situation; until, that is, one of the women suddenly stood up in the middle and started dancing, revealing an inner verve and invincible determination: '*We! mshlamane uzungakholwa*' - 'Hey! Pretoria, my "friend"! Don't forget. We'll get our land back'.

SONGS OF LIBERATION AND PROTEST

Until recently the popular image of South African resistance has been acts of sabotage carried out by umKhonto weSizwe, the armed wing of the ANC, and 'rioting' blacks in the townships. It is perhaps only since the Defiance Campaign in 1989 and the growing focus on South Africa in the media with the unbanning of the ANC and the release of Nelson Mandela that people have been presented with a more balanced view both of the ANC and the true nature of resistance in South Africa today, which is mainly non-violent. From its inception in 1912, the ANC's aim has been to engage in meaningful, non-violent political dialogue with the South African State to work towards political emancipation for non-whites. Those repeated attempts to gain freedom failed due to the reluctance of successive governments to relinquish political and economic power, a fact which is still true at the time of writing.

Over the decades non-whites have organized series of protests in such forms as strikes, marches, demonstrations, the disregarding of separate amenities, the burning of passes and so on. But there has always been a price to pay for opposing apartheid. Police have reacted to peaceful protesters with sjamboks, whips, dogs, rubber bullets and live ammunition, and more recently tear-gas and water cannons. At worst the army has been sent into the townships, not only turning countryman against unarmed countryman but also against women and children, a factor in the decision of many young whites refusing to join the army in recent years. By September 1989, 771 white men had signed a statement declaring their refusal to serve in the South African Defence Force, risking a maximum prison sentence of six years for conscientious objection.

The cost of opposing apartheid has also been borne by individuals. Community leaders have been arrested and detained for long periods, often without charge, suffering degradation and torture. Others have been harassed, intimidated, their homes raided, phones tapped and letters opened. Some have been banned or placed under restriction orders. Some have disappeared under mysterious circumstances, their bodies later showing up at the mortuary; others have been murdered by vigilantes or hit-men. There has been a tragic cycle of funeral begetting funeral in recent years, as unknown gunmen have shot into crowds of mourners at ANC funerals. Life appears to be cheap.

After the banning of the ANC in the '60s resisters to apartheid had to find other outlets for their political voice. This was mainly achieved through a wide range of community organizations, the trade unions and the gathering momentum of political groupings such as the United Democratic Front (UDF) and in 1989 the Mass Democratic Movement. In addition, during the '80s the churches started to become mouthpieces for the oppressed in a more concerted way (see under separate subject headings).

Three songs in this section I recorded at a funeral in Khayelitsha, the black township on the dusty, windswept Cape Flats outside Cape Town. The following tale is of three young men who are no longer able to tell their own story. On election night in September 1989 Lizwe Power Mlaza (25 years old) had walked his pregnant wife to the clinic and on his way home met two friends. They were stopped and questioned by riot police, nervous of open opposition to the elections that day. When they told the police they didn't know the answers to their questions and continued walking, all three were shot dead. ANC flags and colours were displayed in open defiance by the crowd at their funeral as the church rocked with liberation songs. Riot police waited on the grass outside, and when the mourners gathered for a meal afterwards they were dispersed three times with tear-gas, re-congregating each time until they at last gave up. These young men were just three of more than thirty people killed around Cape Town on election night - the dead included a child killed in the front room of his house by a stray police bullet.

The Defiance Campaign of 1989 was a series of non-violent actions such as meetings of banned groups; rallies which technically constituted illegal gatherings under the Emergency regulations; restricted people breaking restriction orders; banned organizations unbanning themselves publicly and going back into business; protests, marches, stay-aways and many other ways to protest against the injustice of apartheid. The unbanning of the 17 organizations had been effected by the people during this Campaign months before De Klerk made his official announcement in February 1990. Now that the ANC is unbanned there is undoubtedly a fresh impetus in the movement towards democracy. It is a long, hard struggle however as other forces which resist the peace process seek to undermine it by inciting violence within the townships, resulting in the depressingly long list of fatalities at the start of the '90s.

The role of women in the struggle has been impressive. The birth of united women's resistance to apartheid was the extension of the pass laws to women. On 9 August 1956 women came from all over the country to the Pretoria government to express their opposition. Since then, women have organized themselves into groups encouraging and enabling them to cope with the hardships facing them and act powerfully together. This first National Women's Day has been celebrated annually with a variety of events including large rallies with speakers, stalls and artistic presentations. At a rally in Johannesburg I spoke to a couple of ladies from a clothing co-operative who had started out by picking up bits of rag and sewing them together. One of them testified to their courage and profound spiritual strength when she said: 'We've got no-one on our side except God - so they will never put us down'.

Women in South Africa have been compelled to find reserves of strength as their menfolk have been detained or forced to seek work far away as migrant labourers. Often women had to care for children single-handedly and took any work they could find to provide for the family - particularly difficult in homelands, where there is a continuing shortage of jobs. A domestic worker I met, whose husband had abandoned her, had left her children in the Transkei in the care of the oldest child and come to Johannesburg to find work to pay for their survival. The stoicism of such women is remarkable and is undoubtedly what gave rise to the song *Malibongwe: Let the name of the women be praised!*

In addition to their profound strength and endurance in the face of hardship and their commitment to working for liberation, women in Natal have been playing an important role in reconciliation between the conflicting political affiliations of Inkatha and the UDF. Lawrencia Askham, of the Natal Organization of Women (NOW), told me: 'NOW has quite a lot of sub-branches in small places - in Caluza it came about after the Inkatha attacks last year. The women decided to form a strong women's organization. They have co-operatives - they do sewing, knitting, crochet, make fat cakes and sell to school kids... They work with the church groups, women's groups, youth groups and Inkatha women's brigades. They feel a women's group is a community thing. There is a burial fund - when someone dies they look at the immediate needs; food, funeral costs etc. Therefore it was not seen as a political organization, just as a women's group trying to help one another. There are about 400 women in the group. Usually if people know you're UDF they'll shun you - or Inkatha. We are all fighting one enemy - apartheid.' Despite these aims and activities of NOW, they are closely watched by the security police.

Artists, writers and musicians have long played an important role in expressing the people's resistance through paintings and sculpture, photography, literature and song.

12   Popular singers and groups, black and white, have expressed their own and other people's opposition to apartheid through songs ranging from satire to poignancy, from anger and despair to hope and a vision of a new South Africa. Like anything that opposed the State publicly, the hardest-hitting of these were banned and artists were harassed. More powerful than any of these, and probably more lasting in essence, are the community liberation songs that have emerged from the black communities. These songs are short, repeated choruses, usually with a leader line, that reflect a wide range of emotional and spiritual responses to oppression. Anger, bewilderment, frustration, determination, optimism, courage, defiance, expressions of solidarity are all to be found in these songs and the power of their unifying force leaves little room for wonder that until very recently they were all banned.

Over the years a few songs have become 'classics' such as *Senzenina* (to the tune of an old, well-known hymn), *Hamba kahle mKhonto*, and *Rolihlahla Mandela*; but in the main the songs change as rapidly as the circumstances because they are essentially a means of communication sung on any occasion when people come together at meetings, rallies, funerals and marches. After the declaration of the State of Emergency in June 1986 and the subsequent mass detentions of young and old alike, the mood became angrier and many of the more popular songs in 1989 were looking to the armed struggle as the liberating force for South Africa. Parallels can be drawn between these and the imprecatory verses of the psalms.

The sentiments of the songs are not wrapped up in subtle imagery and poetry. Rather the words make bold statements: 'What have we done?'; 'Children of Africa are dying for their country'; 'Release Mandela, he has done no wrong'; 'We are going to bury apartheid'; 'We're being killed by the Boers in South Africa'; 'We follow our Mandela despite detention'. There are many songs about Nelson Mandela and calling for his release from prison. Although he was released in February 1990, these songs continue to be sung because Mandela has become the symbol of the oppressed still struggling for freedom in their own land.

The words of the songs are in a mixture of languages - Zulu, Xhosa, Sotho, Tswana, English, Afrikaans in the Cape, this being the first language of the so-called coloured people, and Hindi, there being a strong resistance movement among the Indian population too. The catholicity of languages is a reminder that the liberation movement is not confined to any one race, tribe or religious group but rather belongs to all who struggle for justice and peace, regardless of colour or creed.

1 NKOSI SIKELEL' iAFRIKA

(Lord bless Africa)

Nguni language group and Sotho

14

Words and translation

Nkosi sikelel' iAfrika
Maluphakanyisw'uphondo lwayo
Yizwa imithandazo yethu
1. Nkosi sikelela, nkosi sikelela
2. Nkosi sikelela, Thina lusapho lwayo.

Woza Moya (sikelela Nkosi sikelela)
Woza Moya Oyingcwele.
Nkosi sikelela, Thina lusapho lwayo.

Morena boloka sechaba sa heso
O fedise dintwa le Matswenyeho
O se boloke (2nd time O se boloke Morena)
Sechaba sa heso
Sechaba sa Afrika
Makube njalo kude kube nguna phakade.

Lord bless Africa
Let its horn be raised
Listen also to our prayers.
Lord bless us,
We, the family of (Africa).

Come Spirit
Come Holy Spirit
Lord bless us, we, the family of Africa.

Lord bless our nation
Stop wars and sufferings
Save it, Lord
Our nation,
The African nation.
Let it be so for ever.

Pronunciation

'u' pron. 'oo'.
'ph' pron. 'p'.
'th' pron. 't'.
'c' pron. as a 'tut' sound.
'a' pron. 'ah'.

Note

1. The first verse of this song was composed in 1897 by Enoch Mankayi Sontonga, a Christian musician from the Cape Province. Over the years it has been sung as a hymn and taken up as the national anthem by various countries in southern Africa and in South Africa it is recognised as the people's national anthem, having been adopted by the ANC in 1925. The last stanza was added spontaneously at a meeting and is sometimes included now. It carries the additional symbolic meaning of the struggle for democracy in South Africa and is often sung defiantly with raised, clenched fists.

2. The Nguni language group comprises a wide range of languages found in South Africa, including Xhosa and Zulu, which are commonly known. The Sotho language group comprises several related languages, the most common of which are Tswana, Pedi and Southern Sotho.

2 INZIMA LENDLELA
(*This road is heavy*)

Guitar: Capo 3
(using bracketed chords)

Zulu

Sung and danced during the taking of the collection at St Paul's Church, Jabavu, Soweto.

Words and translation

Inzima lendlela, inameva, iyahlaba,
Guqu thandaze

This road is heavy, it has thorns, it pricks,
Kneel and pray

Pronunciation

'Inzima' pron. 'in-zee-ma'.
'iyahlaba' pron. 'ee-ya-hla-ba' ('hl' as in the Welsh 'll', eg. Llanberis)
'Guqu' pron. 'Goo-qu' (The 'q' is a hard 'cluck')

Notes

The 'heavy road' is the struggle under oppression in South Africa; this song is therefore understood as a liberation theology song.
It is most commonly sung with the start of each phrase (Inzima or Guqu) overlapping the end of the previous phrase, in other
words, anticipating it by a bar. I've tried to write the rhythm as closely as possible to how it is sung, swung off the beat.
A simpler way to write it is set out below, assuming the anticipation of the beats.

3 UTHANDO LWAKHE
(*God's love*)

Zulu

Words and translation

1. Uthando lwakhe luyamangalisa
2. Sihamba naye, sihlala naye,
   silala naye, sivuka naye.

God's love is a fascinating mystery
We walk with him, we stay with him,
we sleep with him, we awake with him.

Pronunciation

Verse 1 is pronounced 'oot-han-do lwahk-heh loo-ya-man-ga-lee-sa'.
'Naye' pron. 'na-yeh'.
'hl' pron. as in the Welsh 'll', eg. Llanberis.
'Sivuka' pron. 'si-voo-ka'.

Note

This song is accompanied by vigorous hand-clapping on the cross rhythm, i.e. ♩. ♩.

4 THUMA MINA
(Send me)

Zulu

Guitar: Capo 3
(using bracketed chords)

Thu - ma mi - na,___ Thu - ma mi - na,___ Thu - ma mi - na Nko - si yam.

Words and translation

1.	Thuma mina Nkosi yam	*Send me Lord*
2.	Sengiyavuma Nkosi yam	*I agree Lord*
3.	Siyabonga Nkosi yam	*Thank you Lord*
4.	Roma nna Morena (Sotho)	*Send me Lord*

Pronunciation

Verse 1 is pronounced 'too-ma mee-na Nko-si yum'.
'Sengiyavuma' pron. 'seng-ya-voo-ma'.
In verse 4 'nna' is pronounced as 2 syllables i.e. n-na

Notes

1. The song is sung with rhythmic improvisations in the tenor and bass parts eg.

   Thu - ma mi,- thu-ma mi - na

   and also with links to each verse, eg.

   Nko - si yam, Si-ya-vu - ma

2. This song is the most popular version of *Thuma mina* sung in South Africa. It was also sung in the ANC camps outside South Africa, where it took on an additional or different meaning as young comrades volunteered to go on a sortie back into South Africa.

5 TUMELO YAKA HA NKEKE KA E LATLHA
(My faith, I will never lose it)

Tswana

1. Tu - me - lo ya - ka,___ tu - me - lo ya - ka, tu - me - lo ya -
2. U - kho - lo lwa - mi,___ u - kho - lo lwa - mi, u - kho - lo lwa -

- ka,___ tu - me - lo ya - ka ha nke - ke ka e lat - lha,___ tu - me - lo ya -
- mi,___ u - kho - lo lwa - mi, a nge - ke ngi lu la - hle, u - kho - lo lwa -

Words and translation

1. Tumelo yaka, ha nkeke kae lathla
2. Ukholo lwami a ngeke ngi lu lahle

Tswana: My faith, I will never lose it
Zulu: My faith, I will never lose it

Pronunciation

'Too-mel-oe yah-kah, ha nkeh-keh ky laht-hla' ('hl' as in the Welsh 'll')

'Ook-hoh-loh lwah-mee ah ngeh-keh ngee loo lah-hlay' ('hl' as in the Welsh 'll').

Note

The smaller notes are added at a later stage in the song. Sometimes during the chorus the sopranos sing the bass line an octave higher.

6 ABASUNDU NABAMHLOPE
(Blacks and whites)

Xhosa

Words and translation

Abasundu nabamhlope
mababulele kunye,
mabavakalise bonke
baculele inkosi.
Taru bawo
yibanofefe kuthi.

Blacks and whites,
Let them give thanks together,
Let them praise (the Lord) together
and sing to their Lord.
Have mercy, Lord,
Give us all grace.

Pronunciation

A 'u' in the middle of a word is pronounced as in 'put', and at the end of a word as 'oo'.

An 'e' at the end of a word is a separate syllable, eg. kun-yeh.

'hl' is pronounced as in the Welsh 'll', eg. Llanberis.

The 'c' in 'baculele' is pronounced as a 'tut' sound.

'kuthi' pron. 'kut-hi'.

'r' in 'Taru' pronounced as in 'ch' of 'loch'.

7 THULA SIZWE
(Be silent, nation)

Guitar: Capo 3
(using bracketed chords)

With drive
Leader

Zulu

Words and translation

1. Thula sizwe, ungabokala
   uJehovah wakho uzokunqobela
2. Inkululeko, sizoyithola,
   uJehovah wakho uzokunqobela.

Be silent nation, do not cry,
our God will conquer for us / protect us
Freedom, we will get it,
our God will conquer for us

Pronunciation

1. 'Too-la seez-weh, un-('u' as in 'put')-gah-bo-kah-lah
   oo-Jehova wah-ko oo-zo-kun-qo-(the 'q' is a hard 'cluck')-be-lah.
2. In-koo-loo-le-ko, see-zo-yit-ho-la ...
   Ta-ta nants-in-koo-loo-le-ko'.

Note

An alternative leader entry to verse 2 is 'Thata nants' inkululeko' (Take, there is freedom) as follows:

8 TSHOLLELA MOYA WA HAO, JESU
(Pour down your Spirit, Jesus)

With a good lilt

Sotho

Sung during the exchanging of the peace at a service of Holy Communion in St Paul's Anglican Church, Jabavu, Soweto.

Words and translation

Tshollela moya wa hao, Jesu, *Pour down your Spirit, Jesus,*
Dipilong tsa rona, Jesu. *Into our hearts, Jesus.*

Pronunciation

Line 1 is pronounced 'tso-lay-la mo-ya wa how, Zhe-su'.

Note

During the exchanging of the peace in Africa, it is normal for songs to be sung as people move around all over the church.

9 HAMBA VANGELI
(Spread the Word)

Zulu

Sung by the young adults group at Youth Alive, Dube, Soweto.

Words and translation

Hamba vangeli elisha *Spread the new word*
Insimbi edle zinye *The iron that eats others*

Pronunciation

1. 'Edle zinye' pron. 'ed-leh zeen-yeh'.
2. Phrase 3 is pronounced 'ham-ba van-gel'e-li-sha.
3. The i at the end of Insimbi is lost, i.e. Insimb'edle zinye.

Notes

1. For a long time the 'word' was obeying the 10 commandments, living a good life. The 'new word' is repentance and the second coming of Jesus.

2. 'The iron that eats others' is imagery for the new Word lasting over all things, standing firm and always being there.

10 MONATENG KAPELE

(In joy we will be together)

Guitar: Capo 3
(using bracketed chords)

Sotho

Words and translation

Monateng kapele,
Re se re tla kopana bohle.
Motse oo re a hlolohetsoeng
Re se re o bona pejana;
Leha maranyan'a se le teng,
O se o hlahile oa khanya.

In joy, wherever we are,
we will still be together.
The home that we long for
we see already in our minds.
Even if there may be some doubt
it has already appeared and is shining.

Pronunciation

'hl' as in the Welsh 'll'.
'o' long as in 'or'.

Note

The complete song, a missionary translation of the 19th century American hymn 'In the Sweet Bye and Bye', is published in *Lifela tsa Sione*, although the harmonies sung at Zeerust and transcribed above differ considerably from the original.

11 SAY'ILIM' INGQOLOWA
(We are ploughing wheat)

Guitar: Capo 3
(using bracketed chords)

Xhosa

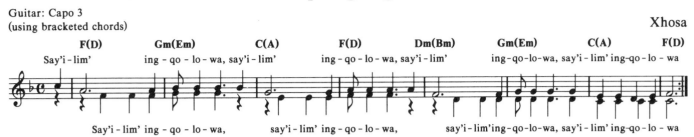

Words and translation

Say'ilim' ingqolowa	*We are ploughing wheat*
Yakhul' ingqolowa	*The wheat grows*
Say' isik' ingqolowa	*We cut the wheat*
Sayibhul' ingqolowa	*We thresh the wheat*

Pronunciation

'Sah-ylim-ing-qo-lo-wah' (the 'q' is a hard 'cluck').
'Yakhul' pron. 'yah-kool'.
'Sayisik' pron. 'sahyi-seek'.
'Sayisik' pron. 'sahyi-seek'.

12 LERATO LA JESO LE A MAKATSA
(The love of Jesus is wonderful)

Tswana

Sung by farm labourers' children in the Child Care Centre run by the Methodist Church in Vryburg, Northern Cape.

Words and translation

Lerato la Jeso le a makatsa   *The love of Jesus is wonderful*

Pronunciation

'Leh-rah-toe Jay-soo o lay a mah-kah-tsah'.

Note
The 'la' before 'Jeso' is not sung.

13 SIKU RIN GWANA
(One day)

Guitar: Capo 3
(using bracketed chords)

Shangaan

Sung by the Youth Group, Ebenezer Evangelical Church 23 July 1989.

Words and translation

Siku rin gwana Hosi Yesu atavuya.
Hina hita yimbelela na Yesu.
Hina hita bokotela mavoko.

One day King Jesus will come (back).
We will sing with Jesus.
We will clap our hands.

Pronunciation

'Sik-oo rin gwah-nah Ho-see Yes-oo ah-tah-voo-yah.
Hin-ah hit-ah yim-be-le-lah nah Yes-oo.
Hin-ah hit-ah bo-ko-te-lah mah-vok-oh.'

Note

The music of the four bars of the refrain is sung to the words of the verse preceding it, with the same rhythmic adjustments.

14 EHLATIN'E LUSAKA
(In Lusaka bush)

Zulu

With drive

Words and translation

Ehlatin' eLusaka
kukhona izingane zama Afrika
ezasishaya
silindele.
Ukubuyel 'ekhaya e South Afrika
ukuyobona abazali kodwa sobabona
ngamhla satholinkululeko e South Afrika

In Lusaka bush
there are children from South Africa
who want to fight
for freedom.
We are waiting to see our parents in South Africa
And we are going to see them
the day we are liberated in South Africa.

Pronunciation

'hl' pronounced as in the Welsh 'll', eg. Llanberis.
All the 'u's pronounced 'oo'.
'th' pronounced 't', except in the 'South' where it is pronounced as in English.
'ezasishaya' pronounced 'eh-za-si-shah-ya'.

Notes

1. 'kukhona izingane' is abbreviated to 'kukhon' ingane'.
2. The final 'a' of 'ukuyobona' and the final 'i' of 'abazali' are dropped.

15 STUDENTE SAL NOOIT VERLOOR
(Students will never lose)

Guitar: Capo 3
(using bracketed chords)

Afrikaans

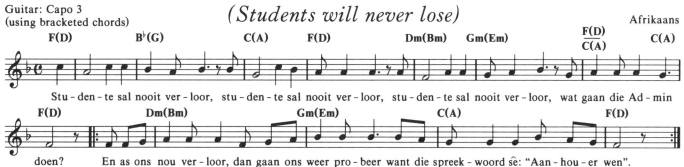

Words and translation

Studente sal nooit verloor
wat gaan die Admin doen?
En as ons nou verloor, dan gaan ons weer probeer
want die spreekwoord sê: 'Aanhouer wen'.

Students will never lose.
What is the Admin. going to do?
If we lose now, then we are going to try again,
Because the saying goes: 'Who persists, succeeds.'

Pronunciation

('St' as in 'step')
'v' as an 'f'
'w' as a 'v'
'g' as in the 'ch' of 'loch'
'ou' as 'oo'.

Note

This is an adaptation of a COSATU song written just before the first protest march in 1989 against racially segregated residences at Stellenbosch University. It was sung during the march around the campus.

16 STOP KILLING OUR CHILDREN

JEAN BENJAMIN

* Play chords to the harmonies specified in the empty bars.

girls of this beau-ti-ful land?— Our sons and our daugh-ters have marched in-to town to bu-ry their

com-rades who have been shot down,— now some are in hid-ing, some man-aged to flee and long for the

day— they can come back to this land and be free.— 5. Mo-ther, where are the

men, where are the wo-men of this beau-ti-ful land?— Some are in ex-

-ile, some are de-tained in so-li-ta-ry con-fine-ment, some on the is-land, some are on death-

chorus transposed into **A**

-row and some have been hanged, *A-lu-ta con-ti-nu-a* in this a-par-theid land.—

6. Mo-ther, where are the sons, where are the daugh-ters of this beau-ti-ful land?

Our sons and our daugh-ters de-vo-ted their youth to fight for our free-dom, for jus-tice and

truth so that lit-tle child-ren in years— to come could have a child-hood—— and a place in the sun.—

CODA

Stop kill-ing our child-ren,— stop kill-ing our child-ren,— stop kill-ing our child-ren.—

WORDS AND MUSIC © 1989 JEAN BENJAMIN

Notes

1. The accompaniment for the verses is picked guitar, for the chorus, strummed.
2. *Aluta continua* is the rallying cry meaning 'The struggle continues.'

17 A NDI BONANGA UMFANA

(I did not see the shepherd)

Xhosa

Words and translation

A ndi bonanga umfana
ukuthi ushone ngaphi
ukuyo land 'inkomo zika Baba.
Iculu seliyana
hamba uyolanda naziya inkoma zika Baba.

I did not see the shepherd.
Where did he go?
It is raining.
Go and fetch my father's cows.

Pronunciation

'ukuthi ushone ngaphi' is pronounced 'oo-koot-oo-sho-neh ngah-pi'.
The 'c' in 'iculu' is a 'tut' sound.
The following letters are 'lost' :-
   The final 'a' of 'bonanga'
   the final 'i' of 'ukuthi'
   the 'i' in 'zika' (pron. 'zka')
   the 'u' at the start of 'uyolanda'
   the 'i' in 'naziya'

18 WE! MSHLAMANE UZUNGAKHOLWA

(Hey! My 'friend', don't forget)

Zulu

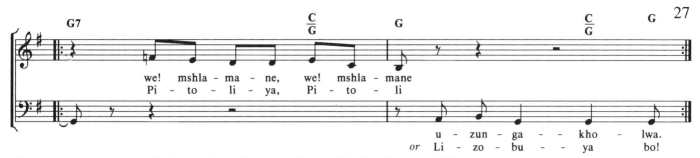

we! mshla - ma - ne, we! mshla - mane
Pi - to - li - ya, Pi - to - li

u - zun - ga - - kho - lwa.
or Li - zo - bu - - ya bo!

Sung at the emergency camp for Zypherfontein farm, near Weenen, Natal on 31 August 1989.

Words and translation

1. We! Mshlamane uzungakholwa   *Hey! My 'friend', don't forget,*
   Lizobuya bo!   *our land will come back*
2. Pitoliya uzungakholwa   *Pretoria, don't forget,*
   Lizobuya bo!   *our land will come back*
3. Amabhunu angakholwa   *Boers, don't forget,*
   Lizobuya bo!   *our land will come back*

Pronunciation

Line 1 pron. 'wem-shla-mah-neh, wem-shla-mah-noo-zun-('u' as in 'put')-gah-kol-wah'.
'Lizobuya bo' pron. 'liz-oh-boo-yah boh'.
'Pitoliya' pron. 'pit-oh-lee-yah'.
'Amabhunu' pron. 'ah-mah-boo-noo'.

Note

The phrases of music and words are freely juggled, the leader indicating the section by the opening phrase.

19 UMZABALAZO
(We are the women)

Xhosa and English

We are the wo - men   We're in the strug - gle
No wo - men, no cry   No wo - men, no cry
Umza - ba - la - zo   Umza - ba - la - zo
Umza - ba - laz', umza - ba - la - zo   Umza - ba - laz', umza - ba - la - zo.

Pronunciation

'Umzabalazo' pronounced 'mzabalazo'.

Note

This song was sung by domestic workers in Cape Town. The words mean that if there are no women in the struggle, their voices are not heard.

20 MANYANANI BASEBENZI
(Workers unite)

Guitar: Capo 3
(using bracketed chords)

Xhosa

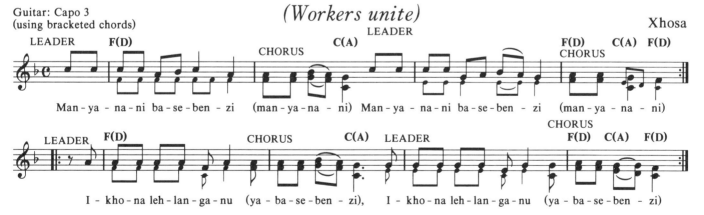

Man - ya - na - ni ba - se - ben - zi (man - ya - na - ni) Man - ya - na - ni ba - se - ben - zi (man - ya - na - ni)

I - kho - na leh - lan - ga - nu (ya - ba - se - ben - zi), I - kho - na leh - lan - ga - nu (ya - ba - se - ben - zi)

Words and translation

Manyanani basebenzi   *Workers unite*
Ikhona lehlanganu yabasebenzi   *There is a fellowship of workers*

Pronunciation

'Ikhona lehlanganu' pron. 'ik-hoh-nah le-hlan('hl' as in the Welsh 'll')-gah-noo'.

Notes

1. This is an alternation of a church song 'Hlanganani maKrestu' (Christians unite).
2. This particular version was sung by members of the Domestic Workers' Union in the Cape. The response to 'Ikhona lehanganu' would vary at the different workers' gatherings, being either the name of the union, or iCOSATU or iUDF(the United Democratic Front).
3. The small notes were sometimes added part-way through the song, either with words or humming.

21 KLIM OP DIE WA
(Get onto the wagon)

Guitar: Capo 3
(using bracketed chords)

Afrikaans

1. Klim op die wa, klim op die wa, klim op SACT-WU se wa,—

Al - mal wat vir SACT-WU lief — het — klim op SACT-WU se wa. —

Words and translation

Klim op die wa, klim op SACTWU se wa,
Almal wat vir SACTWU lief het
2. Hop op die wa . . . .
3. Bly op die wa . . . .

Get onto the wagon, get onto SACTWU'S wagon
Everyone who loves SACTWU
Hop onto the wagon
Stay on the wagon

Pronunciation

1. 'Klim op die wa' is pronounced 'klem op dee var'
2. Line 2 is pronounced 'Ahlmahl vut feer SACT-WOO leef het'.
3. 'Bly' is pronounced 'blay'.

Notes

1. SACTWU is the South African Clothing Trade Workers' Union, newly formed in 1989.
2. The names of any unions are implanted in the appropriate place, this being a popular union song.

22 DAAI STONES
(Those stones)

Afrikaans

1. Die Swar - tes en die Brui - nes werk e - we hard, die Swar - tes en die Brui - nes werk

e - we hard, die Swar - tes en die Brui - nes werk e - we hard, Maar die Boe - re ver - dien daai geld.

Taught to Stellenbosch University students by local farmworkers on the vineyards.

Words and translation

1. Die swartes en die bruines werk ewe hard
Maar die Boere verdien daai geld.

2. Hulle sit op hulle gatte en skryf wette uit
Maar dir Boere verdien daai geld.

3. Daai stones, daai stones, daai riot stones
Die Boere verdien daai stones.

The blacks and 'coloureds' work equally hard,
but the Boers get that money.

They sit on their behinds and write out laws,
But the Boers get that money.

Those stones, those riot stones,
The Boers earn/deserve those stones.

Pronunciation

As in English except:-
Die (pron. 'dee')
bruin (pron. 'brain')
werk (pron. 'vairk')
ewe (pron. 'earver')
verdien (pron. 'feardeen')
gatte (pron. 'chah-ter', 'ch' as in 'loch')
geld (pron. 'chelt', 'ch' as in 'loch')
skryf (pron. 'scraif')
wette (pron. 'vetter')
uit (pron. 'eight')
daai (pron. 'dah-ee')

Note

This popular tune has done the rounds, starting as the American spiritual 'Dem bones, dem dry bones'. It was adopted by Firestone Tyres for an advert on South African television with the catch-phrase 'Your car deserves Firestones'. This song is a witty parody on the advert, which changes to 'The Boers deserve daai stones', becoming a protest song sung by another oppressed group.

23 ORGANIZE AND MOBILIZE

JEAN BENJAMIN

After v.3, go direct from the chorus into v.4.
In the final chorus after v.5, repeat the last
4 bars of the chorus.

WORDS AND MUSIC © 1988 JEAN BENJAMIN

Note

'Organize and mobilize' is one of the common rallying cries in South Africa.

24 SIYAYA EPITORI
(We are going to Pretoria)

Zulu

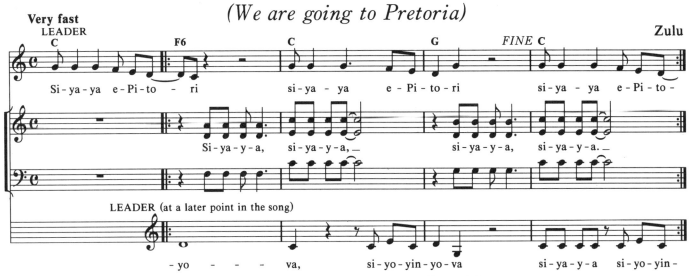

Words and translation

Siyaya ePitori · *We're going to Pretoria*
Siyoyinyova · *We're going to fight them head on*

Pronunciation

'See-yah-yah eh-Pit-or-ee,
See-yo-yin-yoh-va'

25 SENZENINA
(What have we done?)

Guitar: Capo 3
(using bracketed chords)

Xhosa and Zulu

Sung at the funeral in Khayelitsha as the coffin bearing Lizwe Power Mlaza was processed down the church. Also sung during the march for Conscientious Objectors (the 771) in Cape Town.

Words and translation

1. Senzenina · *What have we done?*
2. What have we done?
3. Sono sethu ubumnyama · *Our sin is that we are black*
4. Sono sethu yinyaniso · *Our sin is the truth*
5. Sibulawayo · *They are killing us*
6. Mayibuye iAfrika · *Let Africa return*

Other possible verses

Amabhunu azizinja · *The Boers are dogs*
Ayakufa azizinja · *They will die dogs*
Hamba kahle qhaw'elihle · *Farewell our beloved hero*
(often added at political funerals)

Pronunciation

1. 'Sen-zay-nee-nah'.

3. 'Son-oh set-oo oo-bum('u' as in 'put')-nee-yah-mah.'
4. 'Son-oh set-oo yin-yah-nee-soo.'
5. 'See-bul('u' as in 'put')-ah-wah-yoh.'
6. 'Mah-yee-boo-yeh ee-Ah-free-kah.'

'Ah-mah-boo-noo ah-zee-zin-ja'
'Ah-yah-koo-fah ah-zee-zin-ja'
'Hahm-bah gah-hlay('hl as in the Welsh 'll')
qah ('q' as a hard 'cluck')-weh-lee-hlay.'

Notes

1. In the Western Cape a rhythmic variant occurs; the bars marked with * are shortened to 3 beats, the minim becoming a crotchet, so the song is in alternate bars of ¾ and ⁴⁄₄. The leader entries at the ends of the bars accommodates this by entering on the third beat each time and using the rhythm ♫ | ♪ to the same notes.

2. 'Mayibuye iAfrika' is a common rallying cry in South Africa.

3. In v.5, 'Sibulawayo' is sung twice to each phrase of music, the first 2 syllables taking the rhythm ♫ .

26 AFRIKA

Xhosa

Sung at the funeral in Khayelitsha

Words and translation

1. Afrika
2. Abantwana be Afrika bafel' isizwe — *The children of Africa are dying for their country*
3. Sizomkhulula uMandela — *We are going to free Mandela*
   (somkhulula is an abbreviation for sizomkhulula)
4. Sizomkumbula uLubalo — *We will remember Lubalo*
5. Sizomkumbula uLuthuli — *We will remember Luthuli*
   (somkumbula is an abbreviation for sizomkumbula)

Pronunciation

1. Ahfreekah.
2. Ah-bant-wah-na bay Afrika bah-fayl-ee-seez-weh.
3. See-zom-koo-loo-lah Mandela.
4/5. See-zom-kum('u' as in 'put')-boo-lah Loo-bah-loh. (next verse Loo-too-lee)

Notes

1. In verse 3 different names of political prisoners are introduced.
2. Lubalo was one of Mlaza's friends who was also killed that evening.
3. Luthuli is Chief Albert Luthuli.
4. A melodic variant is below.

27 SONGENA SIRUBULUZA

(We enter crawling)

Xhosa

Sung at the funeral in Khayelitsha

Words and translation

Songena sirubuluza	*we enter crawling*
sizongcwaba iapartheid	*we are going to bury apartheid*
Oliver Tambo, sifak' iFreedom Chart	*Oliver Tambo, introduce the Freedom Charter*
Siyay'e kolony	*we are going to the colony*

Pronunciation

'Son-gay-na sroo-boo-looz ('r' pron. as 'ch' in 'loch')
song-cwahb ('c' pron. as a 'tut' sound) ee-apartheid
Oliver Tambo, see-fahk ee-Freedom Chart
see-yah-yeh ko-lon.'

Notes

1. This is an extended 'siyaya' song - compare with 'Siyaya ePitori'.
2. The 'colony' is the Cape colony, one of the seats of government.
3. At a later stage in the song the bars marked * replace the opening section of the song, picking up again at 'songcwab' iapartheid'.

28 MANDELA PRESCRIBES FOR FREEDOM

Guitar: Capo 3 (using bracketed chords)

Pronunciation

'Rolihlahla' pron. 'Roh-lee-hlah-hlah' ('hl' as in the Welsh 'll').

29 ROLIHLAHLA MANDELA

Notes

1. 'Rolihlahla' is Nelson Mandela's African name. The 'R' is pronounced as in the 'ch' of 'loch'. The 'hl' is pronounced as in the Welsh 'll', eg. Llandudno.

2. Over the years the original version of *Mandela prescribes for freedom* has been modified into this second starker version. The two versions fit together most of the time, with the notable exception of the flattened 7th in bar 5.

30 RELEASE MANDELA

Xhosa

O-li-ver Tam-bo O-li-ver Tam-bo the-ta no Bo-tha a (u Man-) O-li-ver Tam-bo
khu-lu-le u-Man-de-la

-de-la i qa-ba-ne u-Man-de-la i qa-ba-ne u-Man-de-la u zo bu-ya.
-la

A khu-lu-le u-Man-de-la, A khu-lu-le u-Man-de-la.
A re-lease u-Man-de-la, A re-lease u-Man-de-la.

Sung at the National Women's Day rally in Johannesburg, August 1989.

Words and translation

Oliver Tambo theta no Botha — *Oliver Tambo speak to Botha*
a khulule uMandela — *He must release Mandela.*
uMandela i qabane — *Mandela is a hero.*
uMandela u zo buya. — *Mandela will come back.*

Pronunciation

'Oliver Tambo tet-ah no Botha
ah-koo-loo-loo Mandela.
Oo-Mandela qa('q' as a hard 'cluck')-bah-neh
oo-Mandeloo-zo boo-yah.'

Note The names vary in bars 1 and 2, eg. 'Bishop Tutu', 'Comrade _____ (name)'.

31 BABA MANDELA

Zulu

Ba-ba Man-de-la Thi-na si-bu-lawa a-ma bhu-

njani I-yo, I-yo, I-yo, nga-be kwen-ze njani Thi-na si-bu-lawa a-ma-bhu-

-nu thi-na si-bu-la-wa a-ma-bhunu e-South A-fri-ca si-bu-lawa Pa-pa Si-su-lu.

nu si-bu-lawa a-ma-bhu-nu Thi-na si-nu. I-

Sung at the National Women's Day rally in Johannesburg

Words and translation

Baba Mandela — *Father Mandela,*
Iyo ngabe kwenze njani — *hey, what is really happening?*
Thina sibulawa amabhunu eSouth Africa — *we are being killed by the Boers in South Africa*

Pronunciation

'Bah-bah Mandela
Ee-yoh ngah-beh kwen-zen-jahn.
Tee-na sbul-wa ama-boo-n' South Africa.'

Notes

1. This song is commonly sung at funerals.
2. Names of other leaders are superimposed for different verses eg. Papa Sisulu.

32 HAYO O TSHWANANG LE YENA

(There's no-one like him)

Sotho

Nel-son Man-de-la Nel-son Man-de-la Nel-son Man-de-la

Nel-son Man-de-la Ha-yo o tshwa-nang le ye-na.

Note

This song is accompanied by a strong stamping movement on the bar and half-bar. It was sung at the FNB stadium in Soweto at the reception rally celebrating the release of Nelson Mandela in February 1990. The leader sang the names of other prisoners who had also been released, including Thomas Manthatha who, with his wife Barbara, sang this song to me in Birmingham in 1992. The phrase 'Hayo o tshwanang le yeno' was sometimes sung as an answering phrase, the lower notes sung first and then answered a bar later by the higher notes.

Pronunciation

Hah-yoh oh tswah-nung lay yay-nah

33 MANDELA WETHU
(Our Mandela)

Zulu

At a steady pace, with a strong beat

Words and translation

Mandela wethu	*Our Mandela,*
Somlandela	*we follow him,*
Noma siyaboshwa	*despite detention,*
Nase majele	*even in jail*

Pronunciation

'Mandela wet-hoo
Som-lan-del-ah
Noh-mah s'ya bosh-wah
Nah-seh mah-jeh-leh'
('Siyaboshwa' is an abbreviation of 'singyaboshwa'.
It is further abbreviated by the elision of the first two
syllables, 'siya' being sung to one note.)

Note

This song is accompanied by a strong stamp with alternate feet on the first and third beats of each bar.

34 HAMBA KAHLE
(Go well)

Guitar: Capo 3
(using bracketed chords)

Zulu/Xhosa

Sombrely

Words and translation

Hamba kahle wemKhonto weSizwe.
Thina bantu bomkhonto sizimisele
ukuwa bulala ona amabhulu
(or: wona lamabhulu)

Go well, Spear of the Nation.
We, the people of MK,
are prepared to kill these Boers.

Pronunciation

'Hahm-bah gah-hlay (hl as in the Welsh 'll') mkon-toh weh-seez-weh.
Teena bant-bom-kon-toh szi-mi-sell-eh
oo-koo-wa boo-lah-lah oh-na a-ma-boo-loo.'
(In line 1, the 'we' of the first 'wemKhonto' is dropped.

Note

This is one of the ANC's oldest songs. The melody is in the alto and bass parts, and should be projected.

35 PARNA JUNDA
(The Flag)

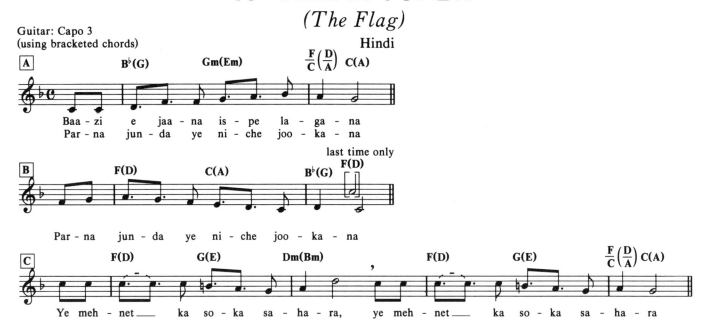

Guitar: Capo 3
(using bracketed chords)

Hindi

Baa - zi e jaa - na is - pe la - ga - na
Par - na jun - da ye ni - che joo - ka - na

Par - na jun - da ye ni - che joo - ka - na

Ye meh - net ___ ka so - ka sa - ha - ra, ye meh - net ___ ka so - ka sa - ha - ra

This song was originally composed in India after the British Army killed thousands of people rebelling against British rule. It is sung today by Indians in South Africa with only one word changed (the original 'jalynaan' meaning 'prisons' is changed to 'galyaan' meaning 'ghettoes').

Words and translation

A	Baazi e jaana ispe lagana	*Bet your life on the flag which shall*
B,A,B	Parna junda ye niche jookana (x3)	*never be lowered*
C	Ye mehnet ka soka sahara (x2)	*It is the refuge of hard labour*
B	Jisne chumka diya hey sitaraa	*It is light and has created stars*
A	Ispe aa-e mooseebuth oothana	*Take up the problems that may fall upon it*
B	Toona junda ye niche jookana	*You must never lower the flag*
A,B	Parna junda ye niche jookana (x2)	
C	Ye muzdooro ke hey ye nishaani (x2)	*It is the symbol of the workers*
B	Jiske durde bhari hey kahaani	*Whose stories are pain-filled.*
A	Ye rahe tho (pron. raho) rahe zindagaani	*If the flag is here, then the spirit of life is here.*
B	Wo jookhe to mitaade jawaani	*If it is lowered, then wipe out the spirit of youth.*
A	Ooska soona hay jo koonka bahaana	*It has heard the flow of blood.*
B	Toona junda ye niche jookana	*You must never lower this flag.*
A,B	Parna junda ye niche jookana (x2)	*The flag will never be lowered.*
C	Jub aazaadi ki bhooke lagiti (x2)	*When the pangs of freedom are felt*
B	To goli galiyaan me chaliti	*then bullets fly in the ghettoes.*
A	Yaadho goliyeka wö aanaa	*Bearing in mind the forth-coming bullets*
B	Toona junda ye niche jookana	*You must never lower this flag.*
A,B	Parna junda ye niche jookana (x2)	*This flag will never be lowered.*
C	Un shaheedo ki kabro pe jaana (x2)	*Go to the graves of the heroes*
B	Phoole aasoo ke unpar charaana	*Shower them with tears and flowers.*
A	Unke hursaal jalse manaana	*Commemorate their lives annually*
B	Jispe khoon ki kahaahi soonana	*On which day their lives of sacrifice are counted again.*
A	Soonke kaapega zaalim zamaana	*And the listeners quiver with feeling*
B,A,B	Parna junda ye niche jookana (x3)	*But the flag will never be lowered.*

Pronunciation
'a' short and open, as in the 'u' of 'cup'
'aa' long as in 'ah'
'e' as in 'get'
'ee' and 'i' as in the 'ee' of 'feet'
'o' is between the 'o' in 'got' and the longer 'oh' (as in the French 'au' in 'pauvre')
'oo' as in 'noon'
'u' as in the 'u' of 'cup' ('durde' is pronounced 'du-r-de')
Consonants as in the English (eg. 'ch' as in 'chum', 'j' as in 'jacket')
except 'th' pron. 't-h'
　　　'ph' pron. 'p-h'.

Notes
1. The song is based on 3 musical phrases, 2 short and 1 long, marked A, B and C.
   The appropriate line of music is indicated in the left-hand margin to the words.
2. 2 notes on one syllable is indicated by 2 dots ¨ over that syllable.
3. As is most commonly found in Indian music, this song is melodic rather than harmonic. The guitar symbols are suggestions only in case an accompaniment is required.

Published by Novello & Company Limited
Music processed by Novello using the Toppan New Scan-Note System
Printed in Great Britain by Caligraving Limited Thetford Norfolk

6/94 (18129)